ANOTHER CRY IN THE WILDERNESS

MY HOMAGE TO EDWARD ABBEY

GUY R. MCPHERSON

**Illustrations
Pauline Panagiotou-Schneider**

Woodthrush Productions/New York/Florida

ANOTHER VOICE CRYNG IN THE WILDERNESS, MY HOMAGE TO EDWARD ABBEY. Copyright ©2020 Guy R. McPherson. All rights reserved. No part of this book may be used or reproduced in any manner whatsoever without written permission except in the case of brief quotations embodied in critical articles or reviews. For information, address **Pauline@woodthrushproductions.com**

ISBN 9798669386412

Also by Guy McPherson:

Only Love Remains: Dancing on the Edge of Extinction

Walking Away from Empire: Second Edition

Going Dark: Second Edition

Killing the Natives: Has the American Dream Become a Nightmare?

Living with Fire: Fire Ecology and Policy for the Twenty-first Century 1st Edition

Applied Ecology and Natural Resource Management

The Planner's Guide to Natural Resource Conservation:: The Science of Land Development Beyond the Metropolitan Fringe 2009th Edition

To the memory of Edward Paul Abbey

Edward Abbey began his short volume of aphorisms with this line: "I write to make a difference." Because of Abbey and a few others who inspired my life and my writing, I, too, write to make a difference. As with Abbey, I also *live* to make a difference. I write and I live to make the world a better place. What does that mean? To me, "making the world a better place" means comforting the afflicted and afflicting the comfortable, as Finley Peter Dunne indicated was the role of newspapers in the 1890s. Dunne wrote for the *Chicago Evening Post* as a journalist and humorist, and his writings were syndicated by *Harper's Weekly* and *Collier's Weekly*. Abbey extended Dunne's idea beyond the human realm, as I attempt to do.

For many years, I have spoken and written about my purpose, and I have asked each of my readers to ponder his or her own purpose as well. I have contemplated the notion of purpose as an individual and also as a member of communities, human and otherwise. These thoughts have been expressed in various outlets, including essays on my blog, interviews with various media, and my books.

As we near the end of habitat for humans on Earth, I believe it is worthwhile to contemplate our roles during the short time we have left. This collection is intended to express my views on that topic, while encouraging others to consider why and how they live.

The structure of this book matches the structure of the book that inspired it. The chapter titles are the same, and each chapter begins with an aphorism extracted from the same chapter in Abbey's book. I retain the present tense for phrases written long ago.

TABLE OF CONTENTS

ACKNOWLEDGMENTS	**viii**
AN INTRODUCTION	**x**
CHAPTER 1	**1**
Philosophy, Religion, and So Forth	*1*
CHAPTER 2	**12**
Good Manners	*13*
CHAPTER 3	**31**
Governments and Politics	*31*
CHAPTER 4	**41**
Life and Death and All That	*41*
CHAPTER 5	**49**
On Writing and Writers, Books and Art	*49*
CHAPTER 6	**55**
Sport	*55*

CHAPTER 7 — 59

Music — *59*

CHAPTER 8 — 63

On Women, Love, Sex, Et Cetera — *63*

CHAPTER 9 — 69

On Nature — *69*

CHAPTER 10 — 75

Science and Technology — *75*

CHAPTER 11 — 81

Money, Et Cetera — *81*

CHAPTER 12 — 89

On Cows and Dogs and Horses — *89*

CHAPTER 13 — 97

Places — *97*

ABOUT THE AUTHOR — 108

ACKNOWLEDGMENTS

I owe a debt of thanks to my friends who reviewed earlier drafts of this collection: Mimi German and Daniel Reich. Enormous thanks are due my friend, and Edward Abbey's friend, Doug Peacock. My partner, friend, and lover Pauline Panagiotou Schneider reviewed the manuscript and prepared the artwork.

AN INTRODUCTION

Edward Abbey was a writer, public speaker, and radical environmentalist who spent most of his life in Tucson, Arizona. His final book was completed about two weeks before his death in March of 1989. Abbey died about six weeks before I relocated to Tucson, Arizona as an Assistant Professor at the University of Arizona. I was to spend 20 years at that institution before voluntarily opting out of my privileged position on 1 May 2009 (fittingly, the day workers are celebrated throughout the world, with the notable exception of the USA). During my two decades of life in Tucson, I became a writer, public speaker, and radical environmentalist.

About two weeks before he died, Abbey completed his 1989 book of aphorisms, *A Voice Crying in the Wilderness (Vox Clamantis in Deserto): Notes from a Secret Journal.* I read the book shortly after it was published, as with nearly all of Abbey's books. I picked it up again some three decades later, more than 11 years after opting out of the corrupt academic system of which I was a part for much of my adult life. As I was reading the book for the second time in the summer of 2020, I concluded that I could pay homage to Abbey with a book of my own aphorisms. After all, my writings and my life were influenced by Abbey from my days as an undergraduate student in the forestry program at the University of Idaho in 1980. This short volume is therefore inspired by Edward Abbey, and also dedicated to his memory.

Abbey's aphorisms were extracted from the "secret journal" mentioned in the subtitle of his final book. In fact, the source was a 21-volume series of personal journals he kept during the last 41 years of his life. In contrast, the collection of aphorisms presented herein is extracted from my public blog, *Nature Bats Last* (guymcpherson.com). For the most part, I have mined my public writings for these pithy expressions, posted at *Nature Bats Last* since August of 2007 (occasionally with minor revisions). I make no claim that my writing rivals that of Abbey. As with Abbey's final work, this book contains a dedication, an introduction, and 13 chapters. My 13 chapters use the titles provided by Abbey in his 13 chapters, and each chapter begins with an expression from Abbey's chapter (for example, my first chapter begins with an aphorism from the first chapter of Abbey's last book).

These aphorisms and the ideas behind them served as the basis for my many public presentations, as well as the books I have written. As a result, regular followers of my work will recognize these ideas and perhaps even the words used to express them.

As Abbey indicated in the Introduction to *A Voice Crying in the Wilderness:* "*Vox Clamantis in Deserto* is a role that few care to play, but I find pleasure in it. The voice crying from the desert, with its righteous assumption of enlightenment, tends to grate on the nerves of the multitude. But it is mine. I've had to learn to live within a constant blizzard of abuse from book reviewers, literary critics, newspaper columnists, letter writers, and fellow authors."

I understand these sentiments quite well. Although my work is not nearly as well-known as Abbey's, I, too, have learned to live with the typical responses to my work: betrayal, derision, rejection, isolation, defamation, and plagiarism. My voice hollering from the wilderness had even less impact than Abbey's voice crying from the desert. As with Abbey, I have no control over the response to my public work. Abbey continues: "But there are some rewards as well: The immense satisfaction, for example, of speaking out in plain blunt language on matters that the majority of American authors are too tired, timid, or temporizing even to allow themselves to think about. To challenge the taboo—that has always been a special delight of mine—and though all respectable and official and institutional voices condemn me, a million others think otherwise and continue to buy my books, paying my bills and financing my primrose path over the hill and down the far side to an early grave." In my case, I am about a million others shy of "a million others" that "think otherwise and continue to buy my books, paying my bills and financing my primrose path." I have a few avid supporters, for which I am grateful. In addition, I have evidence on my side. As a result, I do not need a million supporters paying my bills. I continue to get by with a few dozen supporters as I near the end of a life characterized, paradoxically, by privilege and also by frugality.

As pointed out in Abbey's Introduction: "The *Deserto* in the title, therefore, denotes not the regions of dry climate and low rainfall on our pillaged planet but, rather, the arid wastes of our contemporary techno-industrial greed-and-power culture; not the clean outback lands of sand, rock, cactus, buzzard, and scorpion, but, rather, the barren neon wilderness and asphalt jungle of the modern urbanized nightmare in which New Age man, eyes hooded, ears plugged, nerves drugged, cannot even get a decent night's sleep."

Abbey loved the physical desert, as do I, for reasons including silence, harshness, beauty, and solitude. He also loved casting the proverbial cool shadow onto the arid, intellectual wasteland into which we were all born.

Few appreciate the rain when it falls, even in the deserts of the world. As a long-time resident of the Sonoran Desert, I came to appreciate the rare precipitation event.

How rare? In my experience, only those fortunate enough to dwell in the desert call rainfall an "event."

As I have pointed out in my recent writings, I write primarily for myself. Abbey expressed similar sentiments. Although I greatly appreciate the support of my followers, and I especially appreciate those few who read my writings, the following aphorisms in particular are intended for me. They reflect my personal, public thoughts, some of which are now more than a decade behind me. I still agree with some of them.

ANOTHER VOICE CRYING IN THE WILDERNESS

*Guy McPherson in Cathedral cum Pub while on
2015 Speaking Tour in Europe*

CHAPTER 1

Philosophy, Religion, and So Forth

The world is older and bigger than we are. This is a hard truth for some folks to swallow. (Edward Abbey)

I must warn you: I'm an equal-opportunity offender with a passion for stirring the societal stew. Edward Abbey, the iconoclastic author from Tucson, was fond of saying society is like a stew: if you don't stir it up every now and then, the scum rises to the top. Clearly, we've needed a lot more stirring since we lost Cactus Ed's voice in 1989.

I am often accused — or credited, depending on one's perspective — of leading an authentic life. As nearly as I can tell, the accusation or accolade refers to the following definition from Merriam and Webster: true to one's own personality, spirit, or character.

When three out of five self-proclaimed followers of a poor, homeless prophet who dedicated his life to working with the poor believe they are *entitled* to wealth, it's no wonder you don't hear much about the common good these days.

Some doors are closed.

Evolution drives us to breed, drives us to procreate, and drives us to accumulate resources. Evolution always pushes us toward the brink, and culture piles on, hurling us into the abyss.

German philosopher Arthur Schopenhauer famously defined happiness as the alleviation of suffering, implying a temporary condition. If the alleviation of suffering qualifies as happiness, then it seems wearing shoes that are two sizes too small is a great strategy for producing happiness, if only at the end of the day when the shoes are removed from one's feet.

As my perspective broadened, so did my expectations for students. My mission to impart knowledge was transformed into a mission to enhance the acquisition of wisdom. Professional employment for every student — the goal of university administrators everywhere — was replaced with my goal, instilling in every student the desire to pursue excellence.

My own educational experiences provided no clues that philosophy and conservation biology were old acquaintances. I was determined to ensure that my students would not leave the university as ignorant as I entered it.

Confined to separate quarters, science and philosophy barely speak to each other in the 21st century. Casual observers would never know they once looked alike, as evidenced by treatment of the two entities on university campuses: compartmentalization is the order of the day.

Most informed readers likely would categorize me as an Existentialist. After all, Existentialism acknowledges the darkly humorous nothingness of humanity. It is simultaneously underlain by absurdity and integrity: The lucid acknowledgement of the meaninglessness of existence leads to the notion that all things are absurd, whereas integrity results from the insistence upon continuing to act compassionately and thoughtfully in the face of the void. I sometimes refer to Eastern philosophies such as Buddhism and Hinduism in calling this approach right action, albeit without attachment to the outcome.

We're part of the multiverse. The continuum rolls on.

My personal philosophy extended to my teaching in classrooms and my mentoring efforts in coffee shops and on field trips. My passion for teaching intersected with my personal philosophy in ways rewarding for me and my students. For example, field trips allowed us to exhibit our passion for the wild and the rare as we bonded from shared, rigorous experiences. This pursuit of a holistic outlook within and beyond the classroom contributed to the development, for me and my students, of eclectic, well-rounded lives.

Science has not lost its way, but scientists have.

For rationalists, the burden of reality is shouldered as one consequence of reason.

We are in the midst of abrupt, irreversible climate change. We are in the midst of a Mass Extinction Event on Earth. So, then, how shall we act? What moral code(s) can guide us? These two questions form the basis for my ongoing work, which I occasionally refer to as Planetary Hospice.

I do not believe in god(s). In fact, I used to tell my students pursuing one of the Abrahamic religions that I believed in one fewer god than they did. I would occasionally mention the 33 trillion Hindu gods, much to the surprise of my students. I used to rabidly deny my religious spirituality. I still do.

If you want to know what came before infinity, then you don't understand infinity.

Science specifically adheres to the idea that knowledge can be discovered and understood. This knowledge is rooted in facts, hence truth (please notice the lowercase "t"). As Edward O. Wilson points out in his fine 1998 book, *Consilience*, morals must derive from science.

Many scientists believe they are serving the common good, although they most often are confusing the common good with common culture.

Sadly, the idea of hope has been imposed upon this culture as a necessity for our wellbeing. Hope has been deemed unimpeachably good. Perhaps this is because hope is imperative if the masses are to be kept in their corral.

After more than three decades of frequent self-reflection, I am comfortable in my own skin. I have thought about how I live. I have developed my own personal philosophy, rooted in radical honesty, and I adhere to it.

We do not form decent relationships with resources. Decent relationships are rooted in empathy, compassion, and perhaps even love. Resources are for exploiting. Perhaps you detect the obvious disconnect. If you adhere to the narrative of the dominant paradigm, then perhaps not.

A word to the wise is unnecessary and a word to an idiot generally falls on deaf ears.

The infantilization of the "western" world is complete. If doubt remains in your mind, I suspect your cognitive function is impaired, your personal infantilization is complete, or you are too privileged to recognize and acknowledge your own privilege.

Socrates famously concluded that the unexamined life is not worth living. I'm surprised it took two millennia for somebody — that somebody being Schopenhauer — to realize that the examined life is far, far worse.

The ongoing, seemingly endless cries for hope indicate we have entered desperate times. After all, hope is a mistake and a lie.

According to the Merriam-Webster Online Dictionary, the first definition of humanity is, "the quality or state of being humane (i.e., marked by compassion, sympathy, or consideration for humans or animals)." It is probably quite easy to recall the last time you saw an individual human being displaying those same characteristics. Probably it was you, earlier today.

There is a difference between teaching and learning. A few years in the ivory tower, surrounded by poor teachers who cared little about facilitating learning, illustrated the point to me.

Edward Said wrote, "there is no point to intellectual and political work if one were a pessimist. Intellectual and political work require, nay demand, optimism." … I admired Said for his courage, and I still admire his contrarian views. And, as a self-proclaimed intellectual who is often accused of inappropriately meddling in political work, I am naturally inclined toward optimism. There's no reason to stir the pot if you think the human condition is hopeless.

The American pragmatist philosopher and pacifist William James struggled with the same question every single morning: Shall I get out of bed? I really don't know how he did it … physically, that is: Personally, I'm emptying my bladder into the toilet before I'm fully awake in the morning.

I'm here of my own free will, to the extent I have any free will. I never imagined I would write these words.

During my final decade in the classroom, I took a strongly Socratic turn, asking my students how to pursue a life of excellence. Bound together as a corps of discovery in the classroom, we focused on the six questions Socrates found so relevant to the human condition and a life of excellence: What is courage? What is good? What is justice? What is moderation? What is piety? What is virtue? These questions are as vibrant and relevant today as they were more than two millennia ago.

I suspect our species will depart our only home like a flamethrower in an oil refinery, with a planetary bang and a cosmic whimper.

I turn to Aristotle for my favorite definition of friendship: a relationship between people working together on a project for the common good. Without the common good, we might as well restrict friendship to drinking buddies. The distinction is as clear as that between being a *citizen* and being a *consumer*. Sadly, I suspect most Americans don't know the difference.

Each of us was born into a set of living arrangements over which we have no control. The scorched-Earth policies we have adopted and implemented during the last two centuries have led to the expected outcome: a scorched Earth.

Why am I here? Where else would I be?

Contrary to society's general disregard for the common good, I have to believe that the greatest measure of our humanity is found in what we do for those who cannot take care of themselves: the myriad species, cultures, and yes, even impoverished individuals in our own country, who never stood a chance in the face of American-style capitalism. I have to believe, in other words, that our humanity is measured in our willingness to protect the common good. And, by pursuing and protecting the common good, we become friends in the Aristotelian sense.

This is it. We are it. We are our own heroes, and our own mass murderers. We can accept the cold, hard truth like the Spartans did and stand fiercely against what comes, or we can daydream away our last days with hope. There is no way to escape this jewel of a planet that we turned into a prison and a death trap for all our non-human relatives.

Through high school and nine years of higher education culminating in a doctoral degree, I did not complete a single course in philosophy. I was exposed briefly, superficially, and vicariously to a dab of Karl Popper and perhaps another philosopher or two who subsequently escaped my long-term memory. And yet I earned a Doctor of Philosophy in that least philosophical of majors, Range Science. In my defense, I have been working hard in recent years to fill the philosophical void (not to mention the existential one).

Am I spiritual? Turning to etymology, we find that spirit is derived from the Latin root *spiritus*, literally, breath, from *spirare* to blow, breathe. I believe breathing is important. I believe how we breathe affects our thoughts. I believe the movement of air — that is, the wind — impacts everything from the structure and function of ecosystems to our daily emotions. Without wind of a certain direction and speed, our food supply declines profoundly and perhaps even vanishes. I am a fan of food. Does that make me spiritual?

By the time I was 19 years old, I came to view awareness not as a gift, but as a curse.

What will we leave behind? When humans depart the planetary stage, will we leave in our wake a dead planet? Will we create a Mars-like rock floating in space, as I have suggested for years? Or will we allow the continuation of environmental conditions that allow life to persist? These are the questions that haunt me. These are the questions that bring my humanity to the surface, thus overwhelming my rationalist brain.

My trademark optimism vanishes when I realize that, in addition to climate chaos, we are on the verge of tacking on ionizing radiation from the world's 456 nuclear power plants.

Earth is in the midst of the fastest-changing Mass Extinction Event in planetary history. Earth is in the midst of abrupt, irreversible climate change. Earth is in the midst of a pandemic. I read every day that humans will be fine. We are clever, after all.

~

If a man does learn from his mistakes, then I am surely among the most learned men on Earth.

Guy and Student

CHAPTER 2

Good Manners

I would never betray a friend to serve a cause. Never reject a friend to help an institution. Great nations may fall in ruin before I would sell a friend to save them. (Edward Abbey)

I am forced to conclude that: more than 5,000 generations into the human experience, with the end of humanity in clear view, our shared goal must be ... the common good. And I further conclude that: As friends, we *reveal* our differences, we *appreciate* our differences, and then we set them aside ... for the common good.

Any moment might be your last. As desert anarchist and social critic Edward Abbey pointed out, "nirvana is now." Let's grab it.

Assuming control as a control freak would, I took the wheel.

Americans are particularly adorable. And by "adorable," I mean unintentionally hilarious. Look at what they call news. And work. And food. And thinking. And entertainment. And education. And success. I could go on, as you know.

There is no meaning to our individual lives beyond what we create.

I am not now suggesting, nor have I ever suggested, giving up. Our insignificant lives have never been about us. They're about the shards of the living planet we leave in our wake, if any. As pointed out by Desmond Tutu, "If you are neutral in situations of injustice, you have chosen the side of the oppressor."

Feeling superior does not make one superior.

According to my email in-box, I am about as sharp as a marble. According to this perspective, there is a decent chance I'm merely clueless.

Industrial civilization teeters on the brink. Abrupt climate change is under way today. It is not a problem for the grandchildren. It is a predicament for today.

Teaching involves helping students find knowledge *and* understanding. Teaching guides students to question everything and think for themselves and we all know that institutions of higher learning do not strive for those standards.

What will it take for the people to act? For that matter, what will it take for the people to *notice*?

My time on Earth is short. So is yours. In response, I will continue to focus on love rather than fear. Will you please join me?

The vast majority of people in the world still do not know about the most important issues in the history of our species. They prefer to remain ignorant. Not only do they not know what's coming, they don't want to know.

No man is an island. But I wish some were.

There is a problem with leaving a legacy: We don't know what it is or how long it will persist

Evaluating evidence is difficult. Most people don't bother. Instead, they turn to celebrities, politicians, and public figures. And they don't understand why this behavior represents an example of infantilization.

My generation has put our entire species behind the biggest 8-Ball in history.

All the Socratic ideals are born again in the love we feel ... for each other, for our families and tribes, and for the natural world. Walking a path that honors the planet and ourselves is a responsibility we share, you and I — a responsibility unlike any other in human history. And it is not just a responsibility, but also something more: It is a joy, and a privilege.

Given a choice, I wish I could un-see most of what I see.

When you're dead, you don't know you're dead. People around you feel it, though. It's the same when you're stupid.

Remember when "go to pot" was a bad outcome?

Intellectual risks are disparaged within this culture, a culture that also disparages the fragility of being human. When there's no reward and ample punishment for stepping outside the straitjacket of culture, the straitjacket gains strength.

The usual response to my suggestion of kindness: "Why?"

My customary retort: "Why not?"

I will continue to play the fool in pursuing and promoting evidence, excellence, and love. Clever people know and avoid my folly in a culture characterized by lies, mediocrity, and indifference. After all, it's generally easier to do wrong than to do right. Color me a stubborn, slow learner. That I can look myself in the mirror without embarrassment is small consolation.

Home is where the heart is. This explains all the heartless people at the workplace.

My scholarly work has been vindicated at last, yet I am not even remotely pleased. I never wanted to witness, much less participate in, a Mass Extinction Event and, simultaneously, a pandemic.

I am a lot more cynical and a lot less enthusiastic than I used to be about my tiny role in this grand play.

If we are all going to die – and we are – then how shall we proceed, as a society? If our species is going extinct in the near future – and it is – then how shall we proceed, as a community?

Trying to balance misinformed criticism with reality, I consider how to spend the days ahead.

Every revolution has failed. And if that's not sufficient reason to launch a revolution, I don't know what is. The revolution is dead: Viva la revolution!

Greed won. Civilization won. Patriarchy won. In the process, everybody lost.

My new path presented tremendous challenges for a life-long academic who could barely distinguish between a screwdriver and a zucchini.

I long ago declared myself a court jester, somebody who would comfort the afflicted while the world burned. I am occasionally referred to as a "large child," and I assume the comment is a compliment.

The role of a decent educator typically extends beyond technical knowledge and into the realm of values. After all, as Thomas Angelo writes in a 1993 issue of the *Bulletin of the American Association of Higher Education*: "Higher learning is an active, interactive, self-aware process that results in meaningful, long-lasting changes in knowledge, understanding, skills, behaviors, attitudes, beliefs, opinions and/or values — that can not be attributed primarily to maturation."

Some people add only Christians as contacts on Facebook, which seems a little intolerant to me.

My near-absence of free will, as with other animals, greatly constrains my path through life. My unwillingness to use my virtual absence of free will as an excuse — a "get-out-of-jail-free card" — keeps me on a respectful, loving path. After all, I doubt you'll find an ethicist who recommends we act as if we lack free will. I certainly don't.

We've never visited so much horror on the living planet, and we've never cared less about it.

So many cases of cranio-rectal inversion. So little time.

Is this the only way to live? Is this the best way to live? Do our hyper-connected, high-tech lives lead us along paths of excellence?

A little learning is a dangerous thing. This explains why some people avoid learning anything at all.

The idea of quality over quantity, for any individual, must be balanced by the pursuit of the common good. We must neither disrespect nor degrade others in our quest for adventure. Because we are alive, we take life (and lives). Yet the pursuit of decency asks us to strike a balance between our own individual pursuits and the lives of others (including the lives of non-human organisms).

Why not come together as one at the one time cohesion really matters?

If the ocean liner waits until it is 30 feet away to change direction by 1°, the ocean liner hits the iceberg. We hit the iceberg. It's not my fault, at least not entirely. It's not your fault, either.

I certainly have no excuse to pursue and present evidence, beyond my inability to escape the teacher within me.

I have been described as tall, dark, and gloomy, especially by people in Mother Culture's main stream. I have been called many names, some of them quite impolite. My favorite moniker comes from someone I met on tour: Dr. McStinction.

Whether two heads are better than one depends on the heads in question.

I'm as fragile as a typical human.

If you're still thinking about which seat to occupy before the movie starts, here's a clue: the smoke you smell and the flames you see are not part of tonight's film. The people pointing out the fire in the theater are not extras.

The time for blame has long passed. The time for shaming others has long passed. No blame, no shame: At the edge of extinction, only love remains.

Too little, too late, I have come to realize I'm not very influential after all. It is quite the bitter pill.

Does a terminal diagnosis preclude decency? Respect? Kindness? Does hospice mean abandoning values? Does it translate to hedonism? Does the fact that birth is a terminal illness that's proven fatal in every case mean we need to act as if our actions don't matter? Does acknowledging death preclude living with integrity?

Hubris does not humble others.

I deliver presentations and write about the problems of civilization. It's my version of television. As narcotics go, it's not nearly strong enough.

An overwhelming majority of Americans (and citizens of the world, for that matter) think Earth is a mere stopover for a better future. The future lasts forever, and the destination is heaven. There is no need to conserve this planet's finite materials if the rapture is near.

The pillars of social justice and environmental protection rose from the cesspool of ignorance to become shining lights for an entire generation. And then we let them fall back into the swamp. The very notion that *others* matter — much less that those *others* are worth fighting for — has been relegated to the dustbin of history.

I was influenced by the words of Edward Abbey, although I never met the man. Abbey the desert anarchist influenced my work in the classroom, where I required each of my students to complete a significant piece of art or literature as a major part of their grades. Consider Cactus Ed's sentiments about the intersection of poetry and science: "Any good poet, in our age at least, must begin with the scientific view of the world; and any scientist worth listening to must be something of a poet, must possess the ability to communicate to the rest of us his sense of love and wonder at what his work discovers."

He's his favorite audience. And, simultaneously, his favorite guest.

Rarely does a person in hospice act like a selfish, money-grubbing arse. Being kind is its own reward. A life of service is as good as it gets.

The problem with being a martyr: One has to die for the cause.

As with every doctor, I have a moral obligation to tell the truth. The other alternative is malpractice.

I can find meaning everywhere, in small observations and small acts. I can find meaning, and mystery, in cliff swallows and butterflies, the kindness of strangers, and a child's love. But there's no role for a social critic when civilization collapses.

Fear is rampant. Empathy is rare.

"Dad, we shot your pickup," I said feebly, at 17 years of age. As a result, I learned how to perform rudimentary body work and also how to paint the patched metal on the truck. And nobody except the beloved Ford was ever in serious danger.

Opinions trump evidence in a culture gone mad. The populace cannot distinguish evidence from opinion when the dumbing-down has succeeded. We are there.

American Empire requires three fundamental elements: obedience at home, oppression abroad, and destruction of the living planet.

Perhaps we'll power down with the tranquility of Buddhist monks. But my bet lies elsewhere.

I will continue to criticize society while empathizing with individuals. And I will ask people to empathize, and to feel. Even if though it hurts.

As we each come to grips with our own mortality, we learn who we really are. We learn what matters to us. We also learn who we can count as our friends. If we are lucky, we learn how to be useful. If we are *really* lucky, we learn to dance. What better lessons could we learn, regardless how long we live?

Language and fire are the two major forces leading to destruction of habitat.

I am adjusting to my new roles as the world burns: court jester and psychotherapist. I have no experience with either pursuit, unless playing class clown contributes to the former. But I think Nero had the right idea, creating art as Rome burned. I will create humor while taking advantage of opportunities to comfort the afflicted and afflict the comfortable.

As a product of cultural conditioning, the typical American confuses anarchy with terrorism.

The survivors from the Olmec, Chaco, and Mimbres cultures all chose tribalism when their civilizations failed.

Despite considerable evidence to the contrary, we have come to believe industrial civilization is the only way to live. As we will soon discover, it is the only way to die, at least at the level of our species.

Thinking is hard, so the majority of Americans prefer television instead.

The idealism I displayed in my classrooms was matched and ultimately overwhelmed by the idealism demonstrated by my students. The dogged pursuit of evidence I promoted for more than two decades in my classrooms remains emblematic of my own personal and professional pursuit of excellence. Such efforts have brought no external rewards, as I warned when I described them in my classrooms. And this is reason to abandon neither the dogged pursuit of evidence nor the pursuit of excellence in a culture of mediocrity.

Color me non-judgmental. Continue to fuck the planet and our future, and see if I give a damn.

Saying we fucked the future without offering so much as a kiss is an insult to four-letter words everywhere.

There is no need to wonder when the apocalypse will arrive. It's here.

Swept up in the pursuit of more instead of better, we have become the waves approaching the rocky shore.

That our species is headed for near-term extinction is no excuse to throw in the towel.

People in bunkers might survive a few years. They will be dehydrated, hungry, lonely, and living within a bleak world nearly devoid of other complex life. Their survival will be a day-to-day proposition, with every day more tenuous than the day before, much as it is today for non-human species.

Have we moved so far away from the notion of resistance that we cannot organize a potluck dinner without seeking permission from the Department of Homeland Security?

This civilization, like others, is characterized by endemic racism, endemic misogyny, endemic monetary disparity leading to poverty, overshoot of the human population, accelerating extinction of non-human species, and various other undesirable characteristics.

The only reason I can imagine wanting to retain this horrific system for a few more years is to safely shut down the nuclear reactors that are poised to kill us.

My Socratic approach was successful according to the only metric that mattered to me: real learning. The kind that sticks in your craw after one has fed at the trough of knowledge. The kind that gives a person the ability, courage, confidence, and desire to question the answers. The kind that changes lives, one life at a time.

Civilizations don't grow *or* die. They grow *and* die.

Unlike other civilizations, this version is characterized by the infinite-growth paradigm, nuclear materials sufficient to cause our own extinction via multi-generational horrors resulting from lethal mutations, and also a much quicker means to our end: the aerosol masking effect, otherwise known as global dimming.

The spy who claims to love me wrote to my friend on 19 December 2016: "THANK you for hosting Guy McPherson. I'm afraid the NSA is about to get much tougher on him and a list of others as Trump & Rex Tillerson have asked for specifics. Sorry. I'm only the messenger." [The organized defamation campaign that effectively removed me from public service was completed within eight months.]

I strongly suspect we are the final humans on Earth. In light of this knowledge, will you live more fully every day? Every moment? Will you prioritize your work differently? Or your relationships? What is important to you? Who is important to you? Are you acting *now* as if these things and these beings are important? Are you passionately pursuing a life of excellence? Or are you stuck on the treadmill onto which you were born? Do you reinforce the jail cell into which you were born with bars comprised of societal expectations? Are you pursuing a life of your own choosing, or are the cultural shackles strong enough to control your every action?

With teaching, one never knows if the messages will be received, or in what form.

It is small wonder, as George Carlin pointed out, that idealism lies on the path to cynicism. I was an idealist for more than four decades before I was profoundly fleeced, a process that transformed me into a disappointed idealist (i.e., cynic).

We fucked the planet, and now it's our turn to bend over.

Not only did the boomers destroy the living planet for other cultures and species, but we turned the dynamite on ourselves. All too soon, the jig is up for *Homo sapiens*.

Principled words have been largely ignored. Principled actions have been largely disparaged. Small wonder the wisdom of our "sapient" species has been so brilliantly, cleverly disguised.

To employ a bit of The Boss: "In the end, what you don't surrender, well, the world just strips away." Or, to employ a bit of Zen: Let go, or be dragged. Or, to employ a bit of popular culture: *Carpe diem*. Or, to employ a bit of Nietzsche: "Live as though the day were here."

Is there a better measure of our character than how we face our individual death and the demise of our species?

Fortunately for governments, few citizens are willing to look deeply into any topic, no matter how important. The shadows in the cave are far too comfortable to risk facing the bright light of reality head-on.

Inspired by Kurt Vonnegut's eponymous poem, I offer the following requiem for Earth:

If Earth could sing with a female voice. Her strength would be evident, though her tone might waver.

Could she withhold judgment against one of her own, through all we've done to her, and our brethren?

We lived in her bosom from which we were born for two million years not forsaking our home.

Then we became something different from all we had known, and in the gasp of a breath we destroyed it all.

Can you blame her for judging us, considering what we've done? She gave us every chance to turn it around.

Now we're all done and she's endured our abuse, including pillage, plunder, and rape without any excuse.

All she can sing in that mournful tone is sorrow for the power she unleashed, through us and thus dispassionately onto herself, destroyed by one of her own.

She must ponder how our hubris overwhelmed our humility in concluding about our recent selves: They didn't like it here.

Guy and Alpacas in New Zealand 2016

CHAPTER 3

Governments and Politics

Anarchism is not a romantic fable but the hard-headed realization, based on five thousand years of experience, that we cannot entrust the management of our lives to kings, priests, politicians, generals, and county commissioners. (Edward Abbey)

It ought to come as no surprise that hope has become a religion as powerful as Catholicism during the Crusades. After all, there is nothing to be done about abrupt, irreversible climate change except keep the show going for as long as money can buy pleasure. Promulgating hope is part of the show for which we inherited a front-row seat.

These days, I rarely rely on America's founding fathers for solace. They were terrorists.

Notably, Patrick Henry did not say, "Give me democracy or give me death." Like the rest of the founding fathers, Henry knew that freedom was primary to democracy; without the guiding light of freedom, or liberty, democracy breaks up on the shoals.

The world's best-known collection of dead white guys – America's founding fathers – had much to say about religion, most of it bad. But the mostly ignorant, church-going members of the American populace have gobbled up so many bullshit sandwiches that the fairy tales they've adopted about the religious views of the founding fathers are nearly as grand as the ones they've accepted about spirits in our midst.

If the Deep State exists, then Americans are culpable for the horrors of imperialism. As it turns out, the Deep State exists.

Civilization is a prison.

The prison-industrial complex, like almost every other aspect of American culture, is designed to enrich the wealthy and enslave the poor. Some people claim the system isn't working. Au contraire: It's working as planned, as indicated by the beneficiaries of American Empire.

My heart, heavy as the unbroken clouds overhead, threatens to break when I think about what we have done in pursuit of progress.

I suspect, and I shudder at the thought, that engineers will be necessary to avoid a near-term lifeless Earth. I suspect, and I shudder at the thought, that CEOs and politicians will be necessary. I suspect, and I shudder at the thought, that a multinational effort rooted in civilization will be necessary.

Earth's final civilization turned out great for a few people. Hot showers and bacon were the highlights for many of us. In retrospect, destroying our only home for a few bucks and a BLT was not the swiftest plan we could have developed.

Despite the attention I have drawn from the U.S. government, I don't get hassled at airports. My acquaintances do, though. Oddly, I get TSA precheck without asking.

The pen is mightier than the sword. So is the rifle.

The two dominant political parties in the United States represent the twin cheeks of the corporate ass. If you believe the next person to occupy the Oval Office will improve the situation for the masses, then you do not understand the issue.

Language and fire are the two major forces leading to destruction of human habitat.

American exceptionalism is a myth. American military power, largely supported by willfully ignorant taxpayers, is necessary to maintain American lifestyles, including grid-tied electricity, the modern banking system, and all that follows.

It's time to grow accustomed to chaos as an everyday event.

For those of us who do not comprise the 0.01%, we are all indigenous now. We are all collateral damage on the vicious road to imperialist dreams. We are needed as consumers and cannon fodder. Willfully ignorant of the evidence, we march to the drum of empire because we cannot imagine another way to live. We cannot imagine lives more important than our own. We cannot imagine a species more important than ours. We cannot imagine questioning the dominant paradigm, much less resisting it. We pursue progress, even if it means progressing over a cliff or into the gas chambers.

If we accept that humans played a pivotal role in loss of species and degradation of ecosystems — and both patterns seem impossible to deny at this point — we face a daunting moral question: How do we reverse these trends?

In this country, we initiate terrorism to create terrorists to overthrow governments.

The psyche threatened by the notion of American Empire is the one of exceptional individualism. Most Americans hear daily, from birth, that America is the greatest country ever to exist, and also that Americans have a strong sense of individuality. The latter characteristic is said to contribute to the former one. According to this narrative, the collection of rugged individualists throughout history makes for a country of exceptional freedoms. People in the United States are told this nonsense so frequently they come to believe it! They also typically believe the United States is a democracy or a republic, rather than an oligarchy. They also believe their own president is in charge of important matters, rather than serving as a distraction for the easily and willingly distracted populace. All this seems ridiculous to observers outside the United States of Entitlement. But only because it is ridiculous.

Civilization is properly defined as the transfer of fiat currency from those who have little of it to those who have a lot.

Change is difficult, especially the kind of change that involves one's own identity. Learning is also difficult, in part because serious unlearning is required before anything of significance can be learned. When painted into a corner by evidence, forced to accept the uncomfortable truth, is it any wonder many people choose continued delusion instead? Is it any wonder people will depart the corner into which they've painted themselves, walk over the fresh paint, and then deny the footprints belong to them? Is it any wonder denial is preferred over facts, even when the facts are obvious?

How much is enough? At what point will I be satiated? At what point will you be satisfied?

Perhaps the most exemplary quote comes from arguably the most enlightened of America's founding fathers, Thomas Jefferson. He was referring to Native Americans, but they were merely the best "them" of the day: "In war, they will kill some of us; we shall destroy all of them."

Empires are not benevolent. This world has never had a larger, more effective empire than the current one.

The United States is dominated by a corporate government and corporate media. When greed is your only god, sociopaths assume control. We're there, fully embedded within patriarchal fascism. The standard response of my fellow citizens: "I want more. I deserve more." I occupy the land of the me and home of the crave.

American-style capitalism is properly viewed as the pinnacle of mass murder.

What are the options, after all? We are on a train going over a cliff, and the cabin smells of natural gas. We can ride out the train wreck or jump out, sans parachutes. The banksters in charge have posed a third option: light a match.

I gleefully entered the indoctrination facilities of public education, believing they would set me free.

It's time to tell the full truth. It's time to pursue hospice, with as much honesty, integrity, and compassion as we can muster. It's time to admit that ignoring the decades-long warnings about climate change have led directly to the expected outcome. It's time to comfort the afflicted, which includes each of us.

The typical approach at events targeted at our best and brightest is to inspire them to greatness by telling them that they are this country's most valuable resource. I don't do that, because I think it would scare the hell out of my audience. After all, have you seen what we do to precious resources in this country?

A chain letter is illegal because early adopters steal from future participants under false premises. When this same phenomenon occurs at the level of a nation, it is not called a Ponzi scheme. In that case, the relevant term is "good monetary policy."

Real education makes people dangerous.

We are all in hospice now. Let's give freely of our time, wisdom, and material possessions. Let's throw ourselves into humanity and the living planet. Let's act with compassion and courage. Let's endow ourselves with dignity. Even if all the data and forecasts are incorrect, even if Earth can support infinite growth on a finite planet with no adverse consequences, please convince me there is a better way to live.

We worshiped at the heavenly altar of economic growth, and triggered hell on Earth.

The founding fathers were deists, and they were very clear about the separation of church and state. Had Charles Darwin published the Origin of Species a century sooner, there is little doubt the reasonable men who founded the United States would have leaned even further away from the cross.

Call me quirky — the government's term is terrorist — but I'm a fan of life.

Giving up is not giving in: accepting our fate is not synonymous with jumping into the absurdly omnicidal mainstream. Just because we're opossums on the roadway does not mean we should play possum. Resistance is fertile, after all.

A condom costs less than a dollar. Thirteen trillion bucks will buy a lot of condoms, thereby sparing us the daunting task of shipping our extra progeny into space and having to worry about finding a new planet when we have mined this one beyond all possible of repair.

Considering the history of western thought, it is no surprise we view every element on Earth as feedstock for industrialization. The only question is when we exploit Earth's bounty, not if.

Contrary to conventional wisdom, there are three Chinese curses. In ascending order of direness, they are (1) may you live in interesting times, (2) may you attract the attention of the government, and (3) may you find what you are looking for. Mission accomplished, for me; all curses have found me.

I keep reading that Antifa, which is short for anti-fascist, is a movement. I had no idea decency was in vogue.

I switched my approach in the classroom to one based on a "Corps of Discovery," in which every participant is expected to contribute to the learning of every other participant. We practiced anarchism, in our own classroom-centered way, taking responsibility for ourselves and our neighbors.

This radical approach to teaching puts it all on the line: As a teacher, everything I know, and everything I am, is exposed during every meeting of every class. How can we evaluate our knowledge, our wisdom, and own personal growth without exposing our assumptions at every turn?

Of course, such an approach requires us to let go: to let go of our hubris, and replace it with humility. To let go of our egos, and instead seek compassion and perhaps even empathy

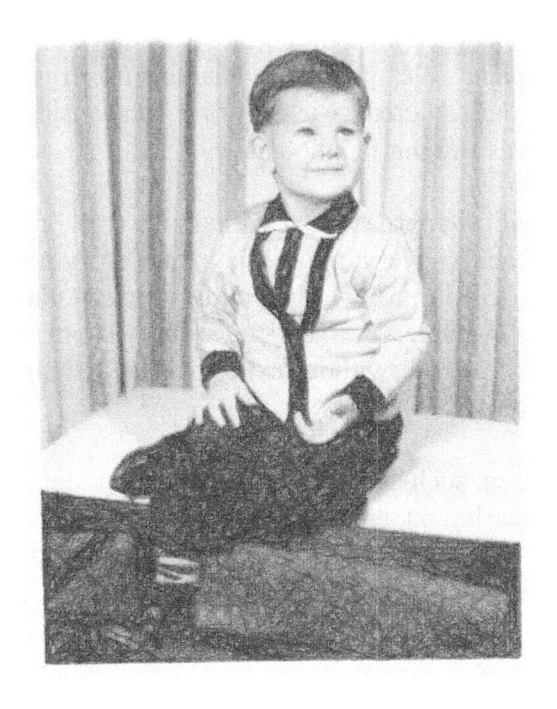

A Young Dr. McPherson

CHAPTER 4

Life and Death and All That

The fear of death follows from the fear of life. A man who lives fully is prepared to die at any time. (Edward Abbey)

The odds against any one of us being here are greater than the odds against being a particular grain of sand on all the world's beaches — no, the odds are much greater than that: they exceed the odds of being a single atom plucked from the entire universe. To quote the evolutionary biologist Richard Dawkins, "In the teeth of these stupefying odds it is you and I that are privileged to be here, privileged with eyes to see where we are and brains to wonder why."

Some of us seek to conduct meaningful lives. However, the universe is unconcerned.

Are there preparatory measures we can take? What must we do, in anticipation of loss of habitat for humans on Earth? What must *you* do, in anticipation of loss of habitat for humans on Earth? What steps must you take to prepare for your own, individual death?

So many questions. So little time.

Until very recently, large-scale die-offs of humans (from the occasional plague, for example) were viewed as "normal," in much the same way we view as "normal" our K-12 system of education, or weekly shopping trips to Safeway, or using a cellular telephone. The description and management of human populations back in the days of the Greek Cynics was oriented along *population* lines, with relatively little societal regard for *individuals*. Humans were viewed as the animals we are, with populations that experience die-offs from plagues and other phenomena. Contrast that perspective with our laser-like focus on individuals.

Birth is lethal.

When you jump off a 100-story building, everything seems fine for a while. In fact, the view just keeps getting clearer as you get closer to the ground.

To an increasing extent, I live as we all must die: alone.

I am surprised any of us survive our teen years. At least in my case, based on my chronically poor judgment, survival was unwarranted.

The wipers swept the windshield erratically and only when I decelerated. The defroster didn't defrost. And every puddle in the pock-marked gravel road shot through the floor boards. Trying to cure these three ills simultaneously with a roll of paper towels led to the expected conclusion. Right before the lights went out, I recall the road coming up to meet my face.

At the edge of extinction, hope is a waste of time.

I once asked a roomful of students, "What was Socrates' most famous quote?" I thought someone would answer with the one about the unexamined life being not worth living. Instead, somebody immediately yelled out, "I drank *what*?"

Will we make it to 2100? I'd give us about a zero percent chance.

Is this it? Will habitat for human animals disappear soon? If so, will your intellectual and emotional preparations suffice?

Earth is done with humans. We're walking around to save money on funeral expenses.

The nun came in behind me, removed the blankets to expose my naked backside, and promptly removed the blade of the Bowie knife previously embedded into my left cheek, the one characterized by the large muscle known as gluteus maximus. The feeling returned in my left leg quite abruptly. My leg afire in pain, the nun waves the broken blade before my eyes and asks, "Is this yours?" My immediate thought: PLEASE PUT IT BACK.

What better measure of our character than how we respond in the face of impossible odds?

Had I known my body was going to last this long, I'd have taken better care of it, particularly during my early years.

As with many artists, my adherence to principle led directly to poverty.

Are we, in the words of English poet Frances Cornford, "magnificently unprepared for the long littleness of life"?

It's too late to meet the three goals I had for myself as a teenager: Live fast, die young, and leave a pretty corpse. I'm too slow, too old, and too late, respectively.

One result of my abstemious existence, as we venture into the dark days ahead, is that I spend considerable time reflecting on my life goals and evaluating — constantly re-evaluating — what I live for.

Cemeteries are quiet, and filled with my favorite kind of people. Is it any wonder I like cemeteries?

Life is short. Life is difficult. Courage demands we act in accordance with reality. Although life is short and difficult, it is beautiful and often even worthy as well.

I know almost everything is beyond my ability to control. I know there are many things I cannot fix. Most of them are beyond fixing, whatever that means. The others are beyond *my* ability to fix, whatever that means. And, as with most of you, I want to leave the world a better place than when I arrived here.

At some point, "the time is near" becomes "the time is here." That time has arrived.

I realize you and I had little to do with the dire straits in which we are immersed. But we will be paying a high price.

I am extremely fortunate to be alive. I am extremely fortunate to have people who love me in this one, small life. I am extremely fortunate to have people who support me and join me on this journey I have chosen. I am extremely fortunate to be living *my* life, and to be in a position to encourage others to pursue theirs.

Remember that everybody dies and that all species go extinct. See. Smell. Taste. Listen. Touch. Breathe. Learn. You want more? Really? To what end, beyond a quick and violent end?

Moments matter. They are all you will ever have. They are gifts of enormous magnitude. Be grateful. Make them count.

What is missing? What remains to be done?

"Remain calm. Nothing is under control."

Hope is hopeless. As Nietzsche pointed out, "hope is the most evil of evils, because it prolongs man's torment." To put Edward Abbey's spin on it, "action is the antidote to despair." Even though I no longer think my actions matter for human habitat, I will take action.

Addictions abound. Freedom awaits. Even if there is no escape from the horrors of empire, even if there is no breaking free from the iron cage of civilization, even if there is no way out of the Alcatraz into which we are born, we can each walk away from the distractions that plague us and that — for many people — have come to define us. If only for a short time. If only for now. If only in our minds. Especially in our minds.

~

I am asked nearly every day for advice about living. I recommend living where you feel most alive and, simultaneously, where you feel most useful. I recommend living fully. I recommend living with intention. I recommend living urgently, with death in mind. I recommend the pursuit of excellence. I recommend the pursuit of love.

In light of the short time remaining in your life, and my own, I recommend all of the above, louder than before.

More fully than you can imagine. To the limits of this restrictive culture, and beyond.

For you. For me. For us. For here. For now.

Live large. Be you, and bolder than you've ever been. Live as though you're dying. The day draws near.

Cover Art by Pauline P. Schneider

CHAPTER 5

On Writing and Writers, Books and Art

Some people write to please, to soothe, to console. Others to provoke, to challenge, to exasperate and infuriate. I've always found the second approach the more pleasing. (Edward Abbey)

Chaos is the absence of rules, anarchism the absence of rulers. As an anarchist, I reject rulers, not rules. I have been clear about this point during more than two decades in the professoriate.

Many of my behaviors made me odd when I was young. Mostly, I suppose, I was odd because I was the principal's kid. As a result, I was one of the few youngsters in town who was often reminded that education might serve me better than a Hobbesian life in the woods. Mom and Dad were both educators, so I read voraciously. Real trouble was hard to find — the meth labs hadn't moved in, yet, and the country's cultural revolution never actually arrived in Weippe, Idaho — so I played outside and, when it rained or snowed, I read books. It rained and snowed a lot.

I am a witness. In bearing witness and reporting the horrors, I do not fit into the dominant culture.

Ignorance is bliss. I need to get me some.

The world is spectacular. It's the humans in the world I find disappointing, disturbing, and — to quote Nietzsche — all too human. Weippe is an excellent example. Overnight, all those FDR Democrats became Reagan Republicans, committed to growth for the sake of growth, the ideology of the cancer cell. They've traded in tomorrow for today by adopting the ideology of neoconservatism (and the cancer cell). And they, along with the rest of Americans, continue to memorialize the world as we destroy it.

I am a teacher, first and foremost. At the age of six, after attending first grade for a few days, I was teaching my younger sister to read. Frustrated when she called the dog a dog, I sputtered, "It's Sp ... Sp ... Sp, Spot!" Rinse and repeat for Puff, whom she ridiculously called a cat. She was four years and a few months old.

After a few visits to the town library, I clearly remember believing I would read all the books. And not merely all the books in the tiny library, but all the books. This fantasy died when I visited the stacks at the University of Idaho library. The melancholy of bittersweet memories returns every time I catch the musty whiff of old texts.

My first book-length work of social criticism, and shorter pieces of similar ilk, made me realize how little society thinks of social critics. It seems the targets of my criticism do not appreciate my criticism. As a long-time welcome recipient of criticism, I was initially surprised. I no longer am.

Considering how difficult it is to change ourselves, we should not expect our words to change others.

My work relies upon evidence. It is rooted in reason. I am a rationalist. Contrary to the cries from my critics, ever eager to attack the messenger rather than evaluate the message, I am not mentally ill. The entire culture is insane. The inmates, who are operating the asylum, believe they are the sane ones.

If you're reading while on methamphetamines, does that make you a speed reader?

Before I made a graceful exit from the Washington, D.C. metropolitan area, I drowned in self-induced misery. One result was my first book-length work of fiction, written as therapy. *Academic Pursuits* was published in 2006 under my fiction-writing pen name, Mac Brothers.

If you are worthy and fortunate, somebody might endow you with that noblest of distinctions by calling you a teacher.

I'm averse to any form of the word "sustain" because we don't and we can't. If the Laws of Thermodynamics aren't compelling enough for you, consider this: Wal-Mart allegedly has poured more money into "sustainability" than any other institution on Earth.

I might be among the last individuals to write social commentary on Earth. Surely there will a prize!

My failure to change society's horrific course has haunted me through the years, as my inner teacher has overridden my Buddhist tendencies. Paradoxically, I've been simultaneously joyous and haunted by the contents of my mind.

In a perfect world, there'd be no need to discuss a perfect world. This helps explain why social criticism matters.

We all know people like him. He's got nothing to say, and he uses a lot of words to say it.

Looking back with the superior vision of hindsight, I would not take this path again. As E.B. White pointed out, "Writing is hard work and bad for the health."

I strongly recommend writing as therapy. It's so much cheaper than a shrink, or even a drink. A superb painting of Minerva occupies the Library of Congress's Great Hall, in the Jefferson building.

A close inspection of Minerva, Roman goddess of learning and wisdom (and occasionally peace), reveals the cost of civilization: Recognizing that civilization requires oppression, hence war, Minerva carries a spear and is accompanied by a shield.

For my first decade as a social critic, my opinion pieces focused on various aspects of faith-based junk science, including creationism, illiteracy, denial of global climate change, and denial of limits to growth.

~

During troubled times, it is easy to forget how fortunate we are. After all, we get to die. This simple fact alone is cause for celebration because it indicates that we get to live. Personally, I love life, and also my own life.

Our knowledge of DNA assures us that the odds of any one of us existing are greater than the odds against being a particular grain of sand on all the world's beaches.

It is really quite a deal. We get to live. Let's live. Let's be fully present. Let's live here now.

SPORT

Quarterback Guy Consulting Coach on Sidelines

CHAPTER 6

Sport

Whenever I see a photograph of some sportsman grinning over his kill, I am always impressed by the striking moral and esthetic superiority of the dead animal to the live one. (Edward Abbey)

It's very small consolation to me that, as the home team, Nature bats last.

Speaking of scum rising to the top, my dean keeps asking me to quit stirring the pot. Apparently by pointing out the absurdities of Americans and their self-indulgent lifestyles, university professors threaten to interrupt the money being siphoned away from big-business donors and toward our football team.

So much for assuming control of the situation.

If my actions impact nobody beyond myself, then why bother? Am I merely keeping myself distracted from staring into the existential abyss, and thus acting like those I criticize, glued to my own version of gladiators on television?

I never enjoyed practicing for sporting events, yet I recognized that practice could help ward off future embarrassment on the court, the track, and the fields. My short career as a Division I college basketball player was filled with grueling practices and a few minutes of playing time during games. In the case of athletics and others, my work ethic was pivotal in warding off future embarrassment on the court and on the playing field.

I had something of a fan club at one point in the college basketball season. When the game would get out of hand — as it often did — my drunk brother and his drinking buddies would begin chanting on my behalf. Coach would put me in for a few minutes, and I even earned a spot on the travel squad by the midpoint of the season.

I played cornerback behind my brother's defensive end every game of my sophomore season in high school. We taunted the opposing quarterback to run the ball our way. He rarely did. On the offensive side of the ball, I still remember the two passes I threw to my brother during his senior season. I never expected to relieve the star quarterback during the regular season, but he hit a rough spot so I played a single series. I called my brother's number, of course. And I drilled him between the numbers, only to see him drop the ball. I called his number again, and this time he made the catch and the first down.

I don't think of myself as an adrenaline junkie, although I love downhill skiing, fighting fires, lighting fires, sex, and skydiving.

According to all four gospels in the Christian bible, even the normally passive, peaceful prophet of Christianity got so worked up about usury in a temple he started acting like Bobby Knight on the sidelines of a basketball game.

In my college days, all I really cared about were women and basketball.

~

During one of the first meetings of *Poetry Inside/Out* in the county jail, one of the men broke down and cried. Considering the strong cultural pressure against crying in contemporary American culture *on the outside* of prison walls, you can imagine what it's like to show such emotion in jail.

Another inmate said, "there's no crying in jail."

Right away, with a reference to the 1992 film *A League of Their Own*, another inmate pointed out that crying was banned from baseball, not jail.

MUSIC

High School Marching Band

CHAPTER 7

Music

The best argument for Christianity is the Gregorian chant. Listening to that music, one can believe anything—while the music lasts. (Edward Abbey)

I largely gave up on popular culture in the early 1980s. The only reason I know about music, television, and film is through my students. This second-hand knowledge has served me well, and saved me a lot of time.

Throughout the whole grad-school experience, I was growing older but not up. By all accounts, I was impressive, young and aggressive, saving the world on my own. Nearly five years later, Ph.D. in hand, happiness was Lubbock, Texas in my rear-view mirror. By this time, I could imagine there's no heaven — it's easy if you try.

If I were to pick a theme song, John Mellencamp's *Authority Song* would be the one.

We put death on display in books, magazines, music, television shows, and movies.

Despite my lack of musical talent and general disregard for music, I was honored with the *Jazz for Peace* Honorary Ambassador Award in September, 2019. Among the four previous honorees are United States Congressional Representative Dennis Kucinich, Ralph Nader, and American historian Howard Zinn.

If silence is the perfect music, then we're about to have the (musically) perfect planet. I doubt we'll be pleased with the silence as we slip, one by one, into the abyss of unconsciousness.

The theme song for my radio show was written by a musician from South Africa. He sent me a beautiful, catchy version. Because it was only a draft, he asked me not to share it until he had a chance to "fix it." A week later, he sent the final version. Both versions sounded the same to my untrained ears.

The camaraderie of the helitack crew was enhanced by the risk-taking Vietnam-vet helicopter pilot. He let us choose the music as we flew to the fire.

I grew up listening to country music, before country music somehow turned into something else. The first songs I learned were by Kris Kristofferson. I would spend hours playing each line of Kristofferson's songs, again and again, on my brother's cassette tape player.

As first-chair saxophonist while a sophomore in high school, I was reading the sheet music in front of me, warming up before class began. Second-chair sax player Keif Martin was warming up beside me, playing contemporary music. I noticed he had no sheet music on his stand, so I asked him how he was playing that particular song, which I knew from the radio.

Keif responded, "I'm playing by ear."

At that moment, I abandoned the life and career I had been seeking for about two years: professional musician. My high-school friend Keif Martin saved me a lot of trouble in pointing out that I had no natural talent as a musician.

Handfasting Ceremony 2018

CHAPTER 8

On Women, Love, Sex, Et Cetera

It is time for us men to acknowledge not only that women are vastly superior beings (that's easy) but also that they are—in every way that matters—our equals. That's hard. (Edward Abbey)

What do the words "woman" and "women" mean to you? Keeping in mind your mother, sister, lover, wife, what do women inspire you to do? Do you think of fear? Do you think of love? Do you think of passion? Do you think of righteousness?

Death and dying, grief and grieving, sex and bodily functions are taboo. And once a person is willing to discuss the subject of near-term human extinction, the floodgates open to any number of topics.

Pursue what you love. Pursue a life of excellence. Throw off the cultural shackles. All of 'em.

Living and loving matter. Passionately pursuing useful work and passionately pursuing love matter. Indeed, little else matters more.

He went off half-cocked. She was even more disappointed than he was.

I suspect few people know that *The Population Bomb*, published in 1968, was co-authored. Professor Paul Ehrlich is credited as sole author of the book because the name of the other author was excluded by the publisher. The publisher concluded that Professor Anne Ehrlich, Paul's spouse, could not possibly know enough about the impacts of burgeoning human population on Earth and its ecosystems. After all, she was—and is—a woman.

You might be a patriarch if you have not noticed myriad privileges associated with being a heterosexual, white man. Or if you accuse women of overreacting. Or if you still believe Yoko Ono broke up the Beatles.

Misogyny and racism are outcomes of every civilization. This latest version—the industrial, global model—is no different from its predecessors, except in magnitude. Much of the misogyny and racism is sufficiently hidden from view that many people claim they do not exist. Particularly obvious among the deniers of misogyny and racism are Caucasian men.

I experience a lot of dujà vé: the feeling I've never been here before.

I used to joke that, when I was in college, I majored in basketball and Women's Studies, while pointing out that there *was* no Women's Studies program at my school. I cannot tell that joke today, not because of the #MeToo movement, but because of the justifiable rise of societal sensitivity since the late 1970s.

As with most issues, radicalization with respect to misogyny is a difficult path, discouraged and disparaged by contemporary society. Digging beneath the surface has its rewards. Comfort is rarely one of them.

Clearly, we have not come nearly far enough in our crusade against misogyny. Even a quick dive into recent history reveals countless instances of social exclusion, sex discrimination, hostility, androcentrism, patriarchy, male privilege, belittling of women, disenfranchisement of women, violence against women, and sexual objectification.

In pre-patriarchal societies the word "father" did not exist separate from "mother" (one of the oldest words in all regions of the world). From the time "father" was separated from "mother," the former word represented the image of ruler-ship, consistent with its current meaning.

With respect to misogyny, we ought to be embarrassed as a society. More important, we ought to do better.

I love humanity. It's the people I can hardly tolerate.

There's method to my madness. There is also a madness to my method.

I cannot deny that men and women have differences, an artifact of natural selection. I cannot deny that we are *all* different from one another.

The terms "woman" and "women" are reserved strictly for our favorite species. We do not call dogs, cats, or parrots "women." We call them "females."

Marriage is a product of civilization. It has become embedded within dominant religions, which are uniformly characterized by the "golden rule." Marriage, like gold and the associated rule, is part and parcel of imperialism. Men own their women, and also their children. Non-monogamous relationships are viewed as weird to the point of being dangerous.

Were I driven to accumulate material possessions, I would have made different choices about how and with whom I live.

Some people incorrectly say my partner was looking for a knight when we connected, intellectually and emotionally. It's clear she was instead looking for the sword I helped her find.

The sword is the one carried by every true educator. It is used to remove ignorance and hubris. It exposes evidence, thereby acting as an agent of truth.

I am a huge fan of sex, although it does not have the same appeal it did when I was in my twenties. Furthermore, I am a professional, and it's only sex. As a society, we've been doing it a while. Look where it got us.

The mistakes I made were falling in love and trusting people. I'd do it all over again, given the opportunity.

For now, I can demonstrate the value and importance of relationships, relative to accomplishments. For now, I can be kind to individuals while forcing institutions to do right, even if it means being unkind to individuals who represent institutions. For now, I can serve people by criticizing society.

At the edge of extinction, only love remains.

~

It is interesting, and even a little entertaining, that only humans are called "women." Indeed, the Merriam-Webster online dictionary defines a woman as "an adult female person." The same source indicates that the word is "Middle English, from Old English *wīfman*, from *wīf* woman, wife + *man* human being, man."

In effect, the word "woman" is a derivative of the word "man," and the word "woman" would not exist without the word "man." As if to pour salt into the linguistic wound, the word came into being only about a thousand years ago, long after a mythical god stole a rib from a mythical Adam and placed it into a mythical Eve.

ON NATURE

Sapodillo Falls, Belize

CHAPTER 9

On Nature

I come more and more to the conclusion that wilderness, in America or anywhere else, is the only thing left that is worth saving. (Edward Abbey)

As I wrote in one of my recent books, the problem is not that the road to Hell is paved with good intentions — it's that the road to Hell is *paved*.

The word "resources" is problematic because it implies materials are placed on this planet for the use of humans. We see finite substances and the living planet as materials to be exploited for our comfort. Examples of intense anthropocentrism are so numerous in the English language it seems unfair to pick on this one word from among many. And, as with most other cases, we don't even think about these examples, much less question them (*cf.* sustainability, civilization, economic growth).

You might think non-human species been doing nothing for us, but they've been providing for our own existence. Let's return the favor.

The cry of a red-tailed hawk drew my eye to two hawks flying low over the treetops. Shortly afterward, a brilliant harvest moon scaled the eastern horizon

. Among the renowned quotes in Rachel Carson's epic book *Silent Spring* (1962) is: "The more clearly we can focus our attention on the wonders and realities of the universe about us, the less taste we shall have for destruction." Sadly, as she accurately pointed out in the same book: "Only within the moment of time represented by the present century has one species—man—acquired significant power to alter the nature of the world." The latter quote, including the reference to the male version of *Homo sapiens*, foretells the story of our destruction, no matter how little our taste for it.

Surrounded by Earth's bounty and beauty, transformation befell me.

Earth is my home because I have found beauty everywhere I have lived. I commune with humanity because I love interacting with people. The living planet is my community because I value the relationships I have discovered in nature.

It was such a lovely planet, yet we are such a short-sighted species. Sadly, evolution does that to some species.

As with each of us, I am a product of my DNA and my personal experiences.

My favorite descriptors of the Laws of Thermodynamics: You cannot win, you cannot break even, and you cannot get out of the game. Respectively, the clauses mean (1) energy is conserved (First Law), (2) entropy never decreases, thus precluding perpetual motion machines (Second Law), and (3) it is impossible to cool a system to absolute zero (Third Law).

At school, I am in my element. I am suited to teaching. I am suited to scholarship. I am suited to delivering presentations. I am suited to being interviewed. I am suited to radical discussions, including facilitating the same. I am suited to being outdoors. I am suited to walking through the wilds of nature, from grasslands to forests, and from deserts to jungles. I am suited to gratefully inhaling clean air as I observe undomesticated animals in their habitats.

I started exchanging physical labor for fiat currency when I was about 12 years old. It was miserable work for little pay. Nine-month stints within indoctrination facilities were interrupted by summers spent clearing fields of woody debris, a job called, "picking sticks." In short, forests were transformed into fields by few youngsters trailing behind a "low-boy" trailer pulled by a slow-moving tractor belonging to a small landowner. At the end of the day, my mom would not let me into the house until she sprayed off the first few layers of dirt with a water hose.

Within the last few years, personnel departments at major institutions became departments of human resources. Thus, whereas these departments formerly dealt with *persons,* they now deal with *resources.*

There is a reason you feel like a cog in a grand imperial scheme: Not only are you are viewed as a cog by the machine, and also by those who run the machine, but any non-cog-like behavior on your part leads to rejection of you and your actions.

It seems you are either a tool of empire or you are a saboteur (i.e., terrorist). It's time to invest in wooden shoes.

SCIENCE AND TECHNOLOGY

Bill Nye and Dr. Guy, 2015

CHAPTER 10

Science and Technology

The basic science is not physics or mathematics but biology—the study of life. We must learn to think both logically and bio-logically. (Edward Abbey)

Science is not religion. Science is not technology. Science is not what it produces. Science is a way of knowing far superior to other known processes of acquiring information with respect to production of reliable knowledge.

Is it possible for a scientist to die from a broken heart?

The pillars of conservation biology — speciation, extinction, and habitat — are poorly understood by most scientists, yet they are crucial to understanding and predicting the demise of organisms, including *Homo sapiens.*

Conservation biologists are aware that every species continually dances on the edge of extinction, constantly hovering on the brink.

Are you willing to forgo fully living on Earth for an illusory rumor supported only by faith? Faith, after all, is belief in something for which there is no evidence.

An old axiom indicates we learn from our mistakes. This, of course, is why I make mine repeatedly: I like to really hammer home the lessons learned from experience. I recommend you learn from mine, thereby preventing some of your own.

Rarely have I experienced an epiphany. Instead, I gradually and deliberately reach a conclusion. This approach would not have suited me well, had I been an early-day hunter. Once I reach a conclusion, I am quick to share it, usually because it is based on evidence rather than my intuition. This approach has not suited me well within contemporary society.

I am not attached to any outcome. This makes me capable of finding and accepting evidence, even dire evidence pointing to my own death and the extinction of the final species of human on Earth. In contrast, fear of death and love of power provide compelling motivation to deny evidence.

To hope is to believe in a favorable future. It is based on faith. Faith requires no evidence. Indeed, evidence generally interferes with faith: witness the spiritually religious among us.

My favorite definition of grief comes from the Grief Recovery Institute: wishing for a different past. Had other scientists been pointing out the full evidence throughout their careers, they would feel no remorse about their contemporary actions. Had they lived as if climate represented a serious existential threat during the last century, then their personal actions would have left little or no room to rue the past.

Hedonistic behavior is implied from a patriarchal culture that views death and dying, grief and grieving, sex and bodily functions as taboo topics. The thought of personal integrity never enters the mind of a simpleton focused on public conversation. Paternalism overrides logic, as usual.

I learned as a youngster that a human construct would protect us: science (and its outcomes, including technology). Now, however, I am convinced that reason and techno-toys have brought us to the brink of extinction.

Science has not lost its way, but scientists have. They have been co-opted by objectivity, failing to recognize the impossibility of the task. They are unwilling to sacrifice their objectivity, which they do not and cannot have, in exchange for doing the right thing. Like nearly everybody else, they are unwilling to make sacrifices to serve the common good.

I find it a bit odd — no doubt because of bias inherent in my life as a scientist — that artists have a better understanding of reality than do scientists.

~

Scientists need not live in fear. The same goes for all of us.

As Lao-Tzu pointed out, "Hope and fear are both phantoms that arise from thinking of the self. When we don't see the self as self, what do we have to fear?" Although I recognize and have frequently pointed out that this entire society is based on fear rather than love, scientists could rise above their reactionary response (and so could the rest of us).

Scientists could set aside their personal emotions during their daily lives, in much the way science asks them to do while they are conducting scientific activities. Scientists are agnostic with respect to religion while conducting science. So, too, could their beliefs carry over to their daily lives.

Guy Hiking in Gila Wilderness, 2017

CHAPTER 11

Money, Et Cetera

Growth for the sake of growth is the ideology of the cancer cell. (Edward Abbey)

Loss of one's integrity is virtually everything, at least to me. Integrity is one of few structures, functions, or characteristics that has not been monetized. Small wonder it is so uncommon.

Time flies. Time is money. That explains why my money went away.

My proclivity leans toward the voiceless. I recognize the incompleteness of the monetary system. My long-time appreciation of rarity comes into play (for example, endangered species, the spectacular view at the end of a vigorous hike, and the sorrow of seeing a shooting star, all of which are not capable of being monetized). I know money easily distorts one's values rather than reflecting comprehensive value.

The greatest cost of my understanding the dark side of humans would have been mediocrity, had I chosen that route. I could have easily capitulated to the mediocrity of the masses, and been rewarded as a result.

Something is better than nothing. Of course, if the something is a pile of shit or dead bodies, this is not quite true.

I am profoundly committed to a life of service, a commitment I attribute to my virtual absence of free will. For me, a life lived otherwise is not worth living, even knowing that service is a trap.

Many people believe they are doing themselves a favor by building social capital. I hear this phrase often, and I bristle every time. Employing the root word of a heinous system that developed as the industrial revolution began is hardly a sure-fire strategy for winning friends and (positively) influencing people. The process of "building social capital" equates connivance with decency.

Giving up enormous privilege comes with enormous cost, and truth-teller is not an easy job.

Aye, there's the rub. Evolution demands short-term thinking focused on individual survival. Most attempts to overcome our evolutionarily hardwired absorption with self are selected against. The Overman is dead, killed by a high-fat diet and unwillingness to exercise. Reflexively, we follow him into the grave.

Honesty is the best policy. Unless, of course, there is money involved.

Five seasons fighting fires led to five seasons lighting fires. As a fireman willing to take risks, I once sprinted through a sheet of flames forty feet high, my face tucked into my inner left bicep and forearm.

It took me many years to realize that most people are incompatible. Had I secured this knowledge earlier in life, I probably still would be teaching. Had I realized most people are takers, I would still be drawing a paycheck. But the costs would be great.

We simply print the world's reserve currency in the greatest Ponzi scheme of all time.

I would rather die a pauper than descend into the type of mediocrity that characterizes the culture in which I'm embedded. Barring late-age, adult adoption, I am certain I will.

If I received a paycheck each time I am said to be paid for speaking the unspeakable, I would not rely on personal savings from a frugal life and donations from others to continue my work.

Born into a family of educators, I was wise enough to choose my parents and country of birth in a way that resulted in a life of relative luxury. When I was a child, my parents looked forward to their combined annual income reaching $6,000. At that point, they knew they'd have it made.

I had the brass ring. And I let it go.

No news is good news. Unless an inheritance is involved.

I am a lifelong educator. In fact, the most common insult hurled my way by anonymous online commentators is "lifelong academic."

A penny saved is a penny earned. If you adjust for inflation, you're better off spending it.

At the age of 18 years, I became a Fire Control Aide I for the Idaho Department of Lands. I wore the uniform of the era: leather work boots, a long-sleeved cotton shirt, blue jeans, and a Bowie knife on my belt (the latter for easy access to cut a fire hose).

Getting offered a penny for your thoughts indicates unimpressive thinking.

I'm often asked why I use the phrase, "human community" instead of "community." This is exactly the type of question I have come to expect from individuals who wrongly believe we are the most important species on Earth.

Being born with a silver spoon in one's mouth sounds like more trouble than it's worth.

So far, the going up is worth the coming down. Life's been good to me, so far.

Because war comprises the foundation for America's entire industrial economy, the empire almost surely would sink to the bottom of the already stinking swamp within weeks of an outbreak of peace. Praying for peace makes as much sense as supporting the troops, and both cases of wishful thinking are clothed in lies.

Every man has his price. And it's a lot lower than you can possibly imagine.

Sharing gifts to develop a durable set of living arrangements within a decent human community: If you can imagine a better goal, please let me know.

A fool and his money are soon parted. So, how did the fool get his money in the first place?

The rewards of the professoriate are supreme. You are allowed to live a life of leisure, in the historical sense: You choose the work you do. Through the lives of your students, you experience life and death the wonderful emotional roller coaster of youth. As such, you can choose to remain forever young, if only vicariously.

Earth's final civilization turned out great for a few people. Hot showers and bacon were the highlights for many of us. In retrospect, destroying our only home for a few bucks and a BLT was not the swiftest plan we could have developed.

I doubt most people can even imagine how deep the Deep State goes. A couple of simple online searches demonstrate with ample evidence what few are willing to admit, even to themselves. For example, the CIA employed Gloria Steinem. The CIA turned Jackson Pollock into a household name. The Deep State has tentacles that penetrate nearly every aspect of life in the United States and therefore throughout the industrialized world. The Deep State has been intricately entangled with the corporate media for nearly a century.

Retaining support as a climate scientist is easy. It requires only one act, often repeated. Lie. Lie by commission. Lie by omission.

Now I live for today, rather than in the past of my faulty memories or for the tomorrow that never comes. Call me a slow learner in a culture of *must go faster*. The speed of life, which often approaches the speed of light, is sufficiently exhilarating for me. Finally, I recognize that going faster offers few rewards that matter to me.

~

I keep reminding my dean, and anybody else who'll listen, that one of my favorite quotes comes from George Orwell: "If liberty means anything at all, it means the right to tell people what they do not want to hear." Not surprisingly, my dean doesn't appreciate Orwell nearly as much as I do.

Of course, my dean doesn't appreciate *me* nearly as much as I do, either. Fortunately, if tenure means anything at all, it means the right to tell people what they do not want to hear.

Guy with Baby Lamb, Clyde, 2017

CHAPTER 12

On Cows and Dogs and Horses

The rancher strings barbed wire across the range, drills wells and bulldozes stock pond everywhere, drives off the elk and antelope and bighorn sheep, poisons coyotes and prairie dogs, shoots eagle and bear and cougar on sight, supplants the native bluestem and grama grass with tumbleweed, cow shit, cheat grass, snakeweed, anthills, poverty weed, mud and dust and flies—and then leans back and smiles broadly at the Tee Vee cameras and tells us how much he loves the West. (Edward Abbey)

Early American conservationist and philosopher Aldo Leopold pointed out in his final book, *A Sand County Almanac*, "One of the penalties of an ecological education is that one lives alone in a world of wounds." A world of wounds because an ecologist can see what we are doing to the living planet. Alone because so few people give a damn.

Livestock represent the single most destructive force in the history of western North America.

Destroying every aspect of the living planet is merely collateral damage: There's a lot of money in planetary destruction.

Urbanization and the associated transportation infrastructure have divided formerly large, contiguous landscapes into fragmented pieces. Fires that formerly covered large areas are constrained by fragmentation, and animals that necessarily range over large areas, such as mountain lions, bison, and grizzly bears, have suffered expectedly.

War, conquest, famine, and pestilence are the Four Horsemen of the Apocalypse, as described in the gospel of John. Contemporary society has us pursuing them rabidly.

Allan Savory proposes using livestock to destroy the remaining life in the world's grasslands. If you're looking for a more extreme example of command-and-control management underlain by patriarchal hubris, you might be looking a long time.

Grazing is not the same as blazing, disturbance advocates aside.

Mancha (Spanish for "Spot") was my first dog after I became an adult. She was diagnosed with bone cancer at about a year of age, and she died shortly after her second birthday. When Mancha died, she nearly took me with her. If I'd have had a handgun at my disposal, I would have used it on myself.

People who look a lot like me accrue privileges like horse dung collects flies.

We do not know we have triggered a self-reinforcing feedback loop until it is already behind us. In this way, a self-reinforcing feedback loop is similar to a dog we run over with a car: Mistakes have been made.

Cattle, the most horrific agents of change in the history of the West, are subsidized by a disinterested citizenry and the entirety of nature in the name of financial profit for the mining industry, the second-most destructive force in the history of the West. This arrangement reveals the "gold mine" of two industries, cattle and mining: the owners get the gold and the rest of us get the shaft.

Cattle grazing is the same old bombing-the-village-to-save-it routine with which we are all well-acquainted by now.

Livestock and "sport" fishes are politically "untouchable" despite adverse impacts on native species and ecosystems.

Exactly zero species native to North America evolved in the presence of cattle.

This planet has become so Orwellian that those who collate the facts and pass them along are hated as liars. For example, I'm the dark-horse candidate for Golden Horseshoe liar award.

What do livestock do? They convert plant biomass to animal biomass. Along the way, the animals remove biomass from the land. That's the whole point of the enterprise, after all: convert biomass into a form suitable for human consumption, and stripping the landbase is collateral damage.

Cattle wreak havoc on soil via several avenues, most notably by compacting soil, removing organic matter, increasing runoff, and decreasing infiltration and percolation of precipitation. The wreaking of havoc is not restricted to soil, but instead extends to other organisms.

The Four Horsemen are lurking in the background, obscured by the never-ending, irrelevant chatter of the corporate media. Here's my impression of Fox News: "blah blah blah Britney Spears blah blah blah Threat Level Orange blah blah blah Paris Hilton blah blah blah … Fox News: the only national news source without a liberal bias." The corporate media's weapons of mass distraction notwithstanding, soon enough the Four Horsemen will be riding tall enough for everyone to see. Population-scale rules from two millennia ago will re-assert themselves.

The livestock industry proposes using the single most destructive force in the history of western North America to heal western North America.

I met my first horse when I was a child of about ten years. The horse stepped on my foot. I purposely stayed away from horses for the rest of my life.

As with most of my cohort in graduate school, I spent a lot of time working on the research projects of other students. A contemporary was conducting research on the diet of cattle. This is how I came to stimulate a heifer into shitting by sticking my fingers up her ass.

My second dog as an adult received her name from my primary study system. My constant companion during a life filled with ecological field research and cross-country travels, canine Savanna was an adventurous warrior. I was devastated when the Best Dog Ever died in her sleep 19 June 2013, two days short of her seventeenth birthday.

I was the human companion of natural-born hunter Savanna. She accumulated at least 14 vertebrate species on her list, including a skunk (pure persistence), two species of cottontail rabbit (pure speed), three species of lizard (pure quickness), and a quail — in flight, on a nature preserve (pure embarrassment, for me).

~

The story of how the West was lost begins when silver and gold are discovered in the area. Any area. At that point, the mining company buys all the nearby available water rights and the attendant land (considerable water is needed to extract ore from rock).

The state constitution of all states in the western United States declares that free-flowing water must be used in an agriculturally productive capacity. The mining company, interested only in getting the water to the mine, leases the land to a cattle company. Shortly thereafter, the local river is emptied into irrigation ditches to grow feed for livestock. The water not consumed by cattle is captured a few miles downstream in an ugly reservoir designed specifically for the purpose.

Where I lived in New Mexico, as a typical example, the water is then pumped a couple thousand feet uphill and a few tens of miles horizontally, across the Continental Divide to the site of the ore. This is how Silver City, New Mexico was – and is – supported by decades-old federal legislation.

ON COWS AND DOGS AND HORSES

PLACES

Guy in Citrus Tree, Belize, 2017

CHAPTER 13

Places

I have written about many good places. But the best places of all, I have never mentioned. (Edward Abbey)

I don't harbor any illusions about my freedom. I live in Police State America.

We were free-range children, consistent with the times. We played until dark, which came late during northern-Idaho summers. We bicycled for miles each summer day, we invented games, we fished nearby streams and rivers, and we were unconcerned with personal safety. Mine was a rough, privileged life.

When I was a child of about ten years, I used to lie on the backyard lawn nearly every summer night, staring at the haunting mystery of the starlit sky. The Idaho town of a few hundred people in which I lived produced little light pollution, so with unaided eyes I could see the stars of Pleiades and all the brighter stars. Many of those nights under the stars I wept uncontrollably at my insignificance in the universe.

I was born into the captivity of civilization, although I failed to see the bars on the cage for many years.

During my youth, I was immersed in a culture of extraction and consumption. I was born in the heart of the Aryan nation in a small mining town in the panhandle of Idaho and I grew up in a tiny, redneck, backwoods logging town.

I spent the summer of 1977 on the campus of East Carolina University surrounded by people who looked different from me. I shared a dorm room with an African American student as tall and skinny as I was. He hailed from Washington, D.C. We studied physics, pulled ridiculous pranks on our peers, and played basketball all summer.

As expected, I went to school, where I was a respected scholar and athlete at a small school in a small town. As expected, I went to college, where I was bored, and I spent most of my time having fun.

Driving as far as I could from my hometown while still availing myself of a generous scholarship from the State of Idaho, I pulled into Pocatello in late summer 1978. I'd been looking forward to maximizing the distance between Hicksburg and me. Yet I couldn't fight the tears of fear and loneliness as I drove into the city and approached the campus of Idaho State University.

We live in the Age of Entitlement, assuming we deserve all we unquestioningly consume.

Missing 42 consecutive days of every class presented something of a drag on my grade point average. The fact that my dorm room was the campus hot-spot for partying probably didn't help. Every weekend was a haze of blue haze. I had the opposite of the Bill Clinton experience: I did not smoke marijuana, but I inhaled.

From an academic perspective, the rare days I spent in class with my eyes open were disappointing on many levels.

I graduated from crappy state universities and I worked at one that is among the worst of the lot. And yet, despite poor educational institutions and serious swimming in culture's main stream, I saw the world.

College expenses were covered by scholarships and summers on a helitack crew. Graduate school meant lighting prescribed fires rather than suppressing wildfires. Today's blazes are intellectual, and much hotter than the earlier ones.

At the height of the cold war, I saw U.S. battleships on the Clearwater River until completion of yet another sign of manifest destiny, the Dworshak Dam.

I graduated high school on the Nez Perce Reservation, a small patch of consolation from the destroyers to the conquered.

I grew up in a backwoods burg of a few hundred people. Known now as the first place the Corps of Discovery met the Nez Perce tribe, Weippe, Idaho was a timber town, back when timber was king. My childhood friends had fathers who worked in the woods, felling and bucking the trees that shot down the flumes into the nearby Clearwater River. I was 11 years old when the last log drive in the continental United States was shepherded down the river in 1971 by hardy loggers with caulk boots and black, stagged-off jeans held up by red suspenders.

If my former students are to believed, I changed the lives of many students, one life at a time. I learned from them, and they from me.

When I was 10 years old, I was walking the three blocks to school. Hearing a noise, I looked over my shoulder to see one of the town bullies pointing a rifle out his bedroom window, aimed at the base of my neck. If memory serves, he was 13 at the time. I kept walking, knowing enough to hide my fear. I thought so little of the incident I didn't tell my parents for a couple decades. It just never came up.

Thrown from the Jeep onto my back, I opened my eyes to dark pools of blood. My first thought: "that's not right." My two-sizes-too-small brain was stuck on obvious, with only three words at my disposal.

Working at a major research university required me to live in a in a city, the very apex of empire.

I have lived and work in Lubbock, Texas, in Athens, Georgia, on Cumberland Island, Georgia, in College Station, Texas, in Tucson, Arizona, in Berkeley, California, in the Washington, D.C. metropolitan area, in Cedar City, Utah, in Grinnell, Iowa, in southern, rural New Mexico, in western Belize, and in many other locations. My learning and my teachings continue to extend far beyond my humble dwelling.

A little education goes a long way. Education was my ticket out of Weippe. But I should have stopped at knowing a little about forestry instead of a little about humans, ecology, economics, and limits to growth. I'd be a happy neoconservative, rather than an informed — and haunted — liberal (aka broad-minded, as indicated by my friends Merriam and Webster). I wouldn't know our culture is violent, diseased, broken, irredeemable.

My career was unexpectedly meteoric, partly because I was talented and able to identify and exploit my talents. And mostly, if I were to hazard a guess, because I am a Caucasian man.

On one of my trips to serve on a research panel in Washington, D.C., I saw a plastic banner hanging on the building housing the Bureau of Engraving and Printing. The banner announced new five-dollar bills, which pretty much says it all: The government uses expensive oil to print an advertisement for cheap money.

I would tell a story about Giordano Bruno to the students I had just met in my classes, and conclude by telling them that some things are worth dying for. One of them, for me, was the truth. It still is.

I delivered about ten presentations each year to a wide range of audiences, from student anarchists to the U.S. Department of Defense.

My one-year gig with The Nature Conservancy made me realize how fantastic life in the academy can be, so I decided to return to the life and students I love.

Three days in Venice, Italy have me agreeing with Ernest Hemingway: This is the best city in the world. Amazing food, people, art, and architecture. No cars allowed! Not even bicycles!

Rebellion cannot be meaningfully pursued while one is shackled to an imperial institution.

I departed university life for many reasons, among them to dedicate more time informing the world's citizens about the consequences of the way we live.

More than two decades after I started down the academic path that led to a productive career in the ivory tower — and much to the amazement and criticism of my colleagues — I returned to my rural roots to live in an off-grid, straw-bale house.

I was asked to move out of my office the same month one of my articles graced the cover of the premier peer-reviewed journal in my field.

Recognizing the costs of imperialism, no longer could I tolerate living at the apex of empire, a large city. Recognizing the moral imperative of living outside the main stream, I left the easy, civilized life for a turn at self-reliance in a small community. Recognizing I was doing good work, and doing it well, was insufficient grounds to keep doing it.

Upon graduating from high school, my 6'1" frame carried 165 pounds. I was the epitome of skin and bones, lean from constant athletic events and the associated preparatory training. My red-hot metabolism probably had a lot to do with it, too. Fifteen months into brutal physical labor at the mud hut has me at 6'3" and 168 pounds of callused skin on degenerating bones.

My customary gifts include hosting visitors at the mud hut and delivery of presentations for no charge. Here at the mud hut, I strive to promote and expand the extant gift economy.

I drink pure water extracted from a local well with PV solar and hand pumps. I eat healthy, whole foods, much of which is grown on this property. I burn no fossil fuels during my daily life in a well-insulated, off-grid home. I know my neighbors, human and otherwise, and they know me.

I led by example. Vanishingly few followed.

Today's big task is construction. The still-tender ribs I broke last month working on a similar project remind me to work deliberately as I attach an awning to the cargo container.

Most of us *claim* to tolerate other races, creeds, and points of view. But that claim comes up well short, in many of my experiences. Furthermore, tolerance is not nearly as much fun as appreciation. Here, we *appreciate* diversity in its myriad forms.

I miss the inmates and honors students with whom I was fortunate to work.

As I look out the picture windows of the mud hut this overcast morning, snow-capped mountains in the nearby wilderness provide a stunning backdrop to the last few sandhill cranes in this small valley.

It is not at all clear that my decision to abandon the empire was the right one. I miss working with young people every hour of every day. I miss comforting the downtrodden, notably in facilities of incarceration, every day. And I miss afflicting the comfortable, notably hard-hearted university administrators, at least weekly.

My two favorite titles are Professor Emeritus and Sharecropper.

I built an impressively durable set of living arrangements at the mud hut. We have six sources of water, we grow a huge amount of the food we eat, and the house is off-grid and astonishing.

I live in a small, sparsely populated valley where gifts are the rule, not the exception. I share a small property with a small family of humans, as well as goats, ducks, chickens, and gardens. We are developing a durable set of living arrangements with particular attention to securing potable water, healthy food, appropriate body temperature, and a decent human community. Living in agrarian anarchy in a human community at the edge of empire, I have taken responsibility for myself and my neighbors, human and otherwise.

On the road, there's little possibility to develop a lasting relationship. I throw a Molotov cocktail into the conversation, and then I leave the area.

The older I am, the better I was.

Sleep comes slowly and poorly, as it has since the summer of 1979 when I last logged six consecutive hours of sleep. Even then, my nagging subconscious was trying to tell me something about the empire wasn't quite right.

I have written and said too many times to count that my work at Homestead 2.0 in Belize is focused on my local community. Here, I live off-grid while working to grow food and reminding people that life is short.

I moved to Central America in mid-2016. I drove along the eastern, Gulf coast of Mexico as part of a small caravan. Had I been one of the young men with guns I met along the way, I doubt I would have been so kind to a wealthy looking Caucasian man from the United States.

In the spirit of throwing off cultural shackles, I continue to ponder my own death as a means of living with urgency. The fact that my body is covered with insect bites encourages my thinking about death via Zika, dengue, and malaria. If I have a choice, which seems unlikely, I will have my body envelope torn merely to break another taboo on my way out. I'd rather die between a jaguar's jaws than from a mundane, albeit toxic blend of bugginess.

Belize is hot, humid, and beautiful. The flora and fauna are excitingly new to me. The natives, particularly in the nearby Mayan villages where I spend much of my time, are wonderfully attuned to nature's bounty. They know the seasons and the response of ecosystems to the seasons. They know which plants will alleviate which pains. They know life is short. They act accordingly. I'm trying to follow their lead.

My partner and I use Homestead 2.0, aka Stardust Sanctuary, as an educational facility. Here, and throughout the world by many means, we facilitate learning. Facilitating learning is our mission. Educating others is our shared purpose.

When I began the ongoing process of walking away from the omnicide of industrial civilization, I felt I had no choice. My inner voice overrode outer culture. I have subsequently come to realize that most people born into this set of living arrangements are literally and figuratively incapable of making a similar choice.

Seeing the world, and experiencing its wonders (and its books), led to learning. And that has made me even more odd (odder?), in the eyes of most people, than when I was an odd 10-year-old.

I moved from western Belize to Pleasantville, New York, a village in Westchester County that lived up to its name. What better name for a place from which to deliver my message? As with my prior acts of relocation, this one was rooted in love.

I recognized my accountability within a system gone awry. Even though I was doing exceptional work, and doing it well, I was participating in a morally bankrupt system. The low-hanging fruit of American Empire fully within my grasp, I voluntarily walked away.

~

That's my two cents, undoubtedly overpriced. And you?

ABOUT THE AUTHOR

Guy R. McPherson (29 February 1960-) was born in the small town of Weippe, Idaho. He received an undergraduate degree from the University of Idaho and two graduate degrees from Texas Tech University. He completed postdoctoral work at the University of Georgia, taught for an academic year at Texas A&M University, and then launched an award-winning, twenty-year career at the University of Arizona. During his two decades at the University of Arizona, he spent a one-year leave-of-absence serving as founding director of the David H. Smith Conservation Research Fellowship Program, a program that quickly became the most competitive postdoctoral program in the world. McPherson also spent one-year sabbatical leaves at the University of California in Berkeley and at The Nature Conservancy's Lichty Ecological Research Center near the Gila Wilderness in rural, southwestern New Mexico. Upon voluntarily leaving his tenured position as full professor at the University of Arizona, McPherson created a stunningly beautiful and functional, off-grid homestead near the Lichty Center. After living at the off-grid homestead in New Mexico for nearly nine years, McPherson moved to western Belize, where he lived off-the-grid for an additional two years. Consistent with his evidence-rich message of living where he feels most useful, McPherson moved back to the United States in October of 2018. He now lives with his partner in a suburb of Orlando, Florida.

Woodthrush Productions

https://guymcpherson.com/

Made in United States
Orlando, FL
15 February 2024